Kate Middleton
Duchess of Cambridge

ROBIN S. DOAK

Children's Press®
An Imprint of Scholastic Inc.

Content Consultant
Arianne Chernock, PhD
Associate Professor of History
Boston University
Boston, Massachusetts

Library of Congress Cataloging-in Publication Data
Doak, Robin S. (Robin Santos), 1963–
Kate Middleton Duchess of Cambridge / by Robin S. Doak.
    pages cm. — (A true book)
Includes bibliographical references and index.
 ISBN 978-0-531-21596-8 (library binding : alk. paper) — ISBN 978-0-531-21758-0 (pbk. : alk. paper)
1. Catherine, Duchess of Cambridge, 1982– —Juvenile literature. 2. Princesses—Great Britain—Biography—Juvenile literature. I. Title.
 DA591.A45C365 2015
 941.085092—dc23 [B]   2015008499

© 2016 Scholastic Inc.
All rights reserved. Published in 2016 by Children's Press, an imprint of Scholastic Inc. Published simultaneously in Canada. Printed in China 62
SCHOLASTIC, CHILDREN'S PRESS, A TRUE BOOK™ and associated logos are trademarks and/or registered trademarks of Scholastic Inc.
1 2 3 4 5 6 7 8 9 10 R 25 24 23 22 21 20 19 18 17 16

Front cover: The duchess of Cambridge waving to crowds on her wedding day

Back cover: The duchess visiting Slave Lake in Alberta, Canada

Find the Truth!

Everything you are about to read is true *except* for one of the sentences on this page.

Which one is **TRUE**?

T or F Kate Middleton left university to marry Prince William.

T or F Kate's son George will one day become king of the United Kingdom.

Find the answers in this book.

3

Contents

THE **BIG** TRUTH!

Anmer Hall is one of Duchess Catherine and Prince William's homes.

5 Motherhood and More

How does Catherine balance her public
and private duties? **37**

Prince George Alexander Louis of Cambridge is Catherine's first child.

5

CHAPTER 1

Early Life

Few believed that Kate Middleton would marry a prince. Middleton was a **commoner**. Her ancestors had worked as coal miners and carpenters in England.

In 2011, however, Middleton walked down the aisle of England's most famous church to become the **consort** of Prince William. She had captured William's heart. She also proved to the British people that she had the wits and the poise to one day become their queen.

← Kate once said that, "I really hope I can make a difference, even in the smallest way."

A Normal Childhood

Catherine "Kate" Elizabeth Middleton was born on January 9, 1982, in Reading, England. Her parents, Michael and Carole Middleton, both worked for British Airways when they met. Michael was a flight dispatcher, while Carole was a flight attendant.

The family lived in Bradford Southend, a small village in West Berkshire. In 1983, Kate's sister Philippa, nicknamed "Pippa," was born. Her brother, James, was born in 1987.

Kate lived in the country of Jordan for two and a half years as a toddler.

Three-year-old Kate has fun on the rocks during a family vacation.

8

Kate spent a large portion of her childhood in this house in Bucklebury, Berkshire.

Becoming Millionaires

When Kate was five years old, her parents founded a mail-order business called Party Pieces. The company sold supplies for children's parties. The business boomed, and the Middleton family became very wealthy.

In 1995, the family bought a house in Bucklebury, another small village. They also sent Kate to a private all-girls school called Downe House. The quiet young teenager was teased by the other girls and soon left.

Kate (front, center) with St. Andrews field hockey team in Pangbourne. She continued playing the sport at Marlborough.

Kate was the captain of Marlborough's field hockey team.

Kate next attended Marlborough College. Marlborough is a private school for students aged 13 to 18 in Wiltshire, England. There, Kate studied chemistry, biology, and art. Her new school also offered sports such as field hockey, tennis, and track and field. These were activities Kate excelled at and loved.

Kate fit in better here. She made friends and graduated in 2000 with strong grades.

Entering University

After graduating, Kate took a year off to travel. She studied Italian and art history in Italy. She also volunteered on construction projects and taught English in Chile. She was even part of the crew on a racing **yacht** off the coast of England.

In 2001, Kate entered the University of St. Andrews in Scotland to study art history. There, an introduction to a fellow student would change her life forever.

The University of St. Andrews is Scotland's first university, founded in 1413.

CHAPTER 2

A Royal Romance

The most famous first-year student at St. Andrews in 2001 was a young man named William Wales. This seemingly normal name hid the fact that the student was Prince William Arthur Philip Louis Windsor. William was second in line to the throne of Great Britain. Kate and the prince were introduced soon after classes began in September. It marked the start of a long relationship.

Like Kate, Prince William studied in Italy and volunteered in Chile before entering St. Andrews.

13

Friends First

William and Kate became good friends. Both were good students and loved sports. They were competitive and shared many of the same interests.

In 2002, Kate, William, and two other students moved into a four-bedroom house together. Although Kate was dating someone else, she soon fell for William. By Christmas of 2003, the two were said to be a couple.

Kate and William tried to keep their relationship a secret from the press at first.

Prince William

The son of Prince Charles and Princess Diana, William was born on June 21, 1982. Upon his birth, baby William became second in line to the throne, after his father. Charles is the son of Queen Elizabeth II.

William's early life was unsettled. As children, William and his brother, Harry, suffered through their parents' bitter, public divorce. And when William was just 15 years old, his mother was killed in a car crash.

In 2013, a former newspaper editor admitted hacking Kate's phone more than 150 times.

Life in the Public Eye

As the prince's girlfriend, Kate came under intense observation. People wanted to know everything about her. Who were her parents? What was she like? Was she fit to date the future king?

The first photo of the pair on vacation surfaced in 2004. Afterward, Kate was hounded by the **paparazzi**. Everyone wanted to snap a photo of the shy young university student.

Kate was determined to live a private life. After graduating in 2005, she and William moved to London. Kate took a job as a **buyer** for a clothing store, while William joined the military. Later, Kate launched First Birthdays, a new brand in her parents' company. She helped design catalogs and worked on production, marketing, and photography for the company.

At times, the constant public attention was too much. Kate finally took legal action. The **media** agreed to let her private life stay private.

Kate graduated from the University of St. Andrews with a degree in art history.

A Brief Split

In December 2006, Kate attended her first formal function with the royal family. Together with Queen Elizabeth and Prince Charles, Kate watched as Prince William graduated from the Royal Military Academy Sandhurst.

Then, in April 2007, the couple surprised royal watchers when they broke up. However, the split was temporary. Kate and William began dating again within a couple of months.

Timeline of Kate and William's Relationship

2004

Newspapers publish the first photograph of the new couple vacationing.

2001

Kate meets Prince William at St. Andrews University.

December 2003

Kate and William become a couple.

Engaged

In 2010, Kate and William traveled to Kenya in Africa for a vacation. William loves visiting Africa because many people there do not recognize him. He has said that the continent is like a second home to him.

In Kenya, William proposed to Kate. He gave her a ring with special meaning. It is the same ring William's father gave to his mother when they became engaged in 1981.

December 2006
Kate attends her first formal royal event.

2010
William and Kate become engaged.

April 29, 2011
William and Kate marry.

Spectators cheer and wave the UK flag. Flags made especially for the occasion sported a portrait of the royal couple.

CHAPTER 3

A Royal Wedding

On April 29, 2011, people around the world turned on their televisions and computers to watch Prince William marry Catherine Middleton. (Just before the wedding, Kate began using her more formal name, Catherine.) A million people lined the streets to catch a glimpse of the royal couple on their way to the wedding.

In the United Kingdom, the day was declared a public holiday. People had the day off to welcome Catherine into the royal family.

The United Kingdom includes England, Scotland, Northern Ireland, and Wales.

New Titles

In honor of the marriage, Catherine's official title became Her Royal Highness Duchess Catherine of Cambridge, Countess of Strathearn, and Lady Carrickfergus. William became His Royal Highness Prince William, Duke of Cambridge, Earl of Strathearn, and Baron Carrickfergus. After his father becomes king, William will become the Duke of Cornwall and the Prince of Wales. These are Charles's current titles. Catherine will probably become Princess of Wales, the title Diana held.

Catherine looks at the crowd outside Westminster Abbey as she enters the church with her father.

Catherine's brother, James, gave the royal couple a puppy named Lupo as a wedding present.

Newlyweds

The wedding was held at Westminster Abbey, one of the most famous churches in the world. The guest list numbered about 1,900 people. Those who attended ranged from royals to commoners, from famous to unknown.

Singer Elton John was there, as was soccer star David Beckham. Catherine's family sat in the same section as Britain's royal family. William even invited a former homeless woman whom he had met at a **charity** event.

William and Catherine (front) leave the church with Prince Harry and Pippa Middleton.

People strained to see Catherine's dress. For weeks, the gown's design had been kept top secret. Created by an English designer, the white satin and lace outfit included symbols of England, Scotland, Wales, and Northern Ireland on it. The dress's train measured 9 feet (2.7 meters) in length. Catherine also wore a lace veil crowned with a diamond **tiara**, loaned to her by Queen Elizabeth.

After the ceremony, the newlyweds traveled to Buckingham Palace, the queen's home in London. The horse-drawn carriage they rode in was the same one used by William's parents on their wedding day.

The day was capped with parties thrown by the queen and Prince Charles. At the palace, the bride and groom appeared on a balcony as onlookers cheered below. At the end of the night, fireworks erupted over Buckingham Palace.

The newlyweds smile at the crowds on the way to Buckingham Palace.

Meet the In-Laws

Catherine's in-laws are the highest members of Britain's royal family.

Queen Elizabeth II (1926–)
Elizabeth became queen of the United Kingdom in 1952. She was just 25 years old. The queen is William's grandmother, and the young man had to gain her permission to marry Catherine.

Prince Philip, Duke of Edinburgh (1921–)
When Philip was born, he was prince of Greece and Denmark. He married Princess Elizabeth in 1947. Before the wedding, he gave up his foreign titles and was named Duke of Edinburgh. When Elizabeth became queen, Philip took the title Prince Consort.

Charles, Prince of Wales (1948–)

As the first-born child of Elizabeth and Philip, Charles is next in line to become king. He married Lady Diana Spencer in 1981, but they divorced in 1996 after a four-year separation.

Camilla, Duchess of Cornwall (1947–)

Prince Charles's second wife was born Camilla Shand. Camilla has two children from a previous marriage. She has been married to Charles since 2005. When Charles becomes king, she will take the title of Her Royal Highness the Princess Consort.

Prince Harry (1984–)

His name is officially Henry Charles Albert David. However, everyone knows this popular royal family member as Prince Harry. William's younger brother has been his closest companion throughout his life. He left the armed forces in June 2015.

Queen Elizabeth II (left) and Catherine walk together on their way to an event in 2012.

CHAPTER 4

Life as a Duchess

Although being royalty may seem glamorous, there is a lot of hard work involved. As Duchess of Cambridge, Catherine's chief role is "to support the queen at home and abroad." This means that after her marriage, Catherine became very busy. She appeared at public events with the royal family and on her own. She also chose several charities to support.

One of the duchess's hobbies is photography.

International Travel

One of Catherine's duties is to travel to different parts of the world as the queen's **representative**. Her first trip as royalty took place in the summer of 2011. That July, the duke and duchess visited Canada and Los Angeles, California. As in England, photographers recorded the pair's every move.

Catherine's outfits, hair, and makeup were chief points of interest.

Catherine has her own staff, including an adviser, a secretary, and a hairstylist.

Catherine stops to say hello to a little girl in Calgary, Alberta, in Canada.

Dragon dancers greet the duke and duchess in Singapore.

The following year, the duke and duchess traveled to Malaysia, Singapore, and the Solomon Islands. They have visited New Zealand and Australia, and they returned to the United States. In December 2014, the royal couple toured New York. While Catherine visited a day care center in Harlem, William met with President Barack Obama. At night, they attended dinners and parties held in their honor. They even went to a professional basketball game.

Catherine visits with a child at Naomi House, a place that helps children with serious illnesses.

Charity Work

The duchess is the **patron** of a number of charity groups. Her favorite charities are those that help children or people in the military and those that protect the environment. She also has a special interest in the arts and is an official supporter of Britain's National Portrait Gallery.

The Duke and Duchess of Cambridge, along with Prince Harry, also head the Royal Foundation. This is a group that gives funds to worthy charities.

Constant Observation

As a member of the royal family, Catherine is expected to appear in public. There is no more hiding from photographers and reporters. An online calendar is posted at the royal family's Web site. It lists the public events at which Catherine and other royals will appear.

Many people faithfully follow the duchess's fashion choices. If Catherine is seen wearing a certain style, stores can count on a surge in sales for those items.

Royal Residences

Being duchess is truly a full-time job. However, as with other jobs, Catherine does have private time and vacations. She and William often go back to Bucklebury to relax with the Middletons. The duchess also has two homes of her own where she can stay.

The royal couple's first and primary home is Kensington Palace in London. It is also the official home of Prince Harry and several other members of royalty.

Many members of the royal family have lived at Kensington Palace, including William's great-great-great-great-grandmother, Queen Victoria, and his mother, Princess Diana.

Anmer Hall is close to Sandringham House, where the royal family celebrates Christmas.

Kensington has a long history. William III and Mary II first used it as a royal residence in 1689. Today, visitors can tour parts of this beautiful old house.

Catherine and William's secondary home is Anmer Hall in Norfolk, England. Anmer is a 10-bedroom mansion. Since moving in, the duchess has added her own touches to the place.

Motherhood and More

In December 2012, the royal family announced that the Duchess of Cambridge was pregnant. The news was exciting to many but also important to the **monarchy**. The new baby would be third in line to the throne. It would not matter whether the child was a boy or a girl. This was new. Before the law was changed in 2013, a son inherited the throne before any of his sisters, even if he was not born first.

Catherine suffered severe morning sickness during her pregnancy. This made her very sick to her stomach.

Catherine's son will one day become King George VII.

On July 22, 2013, Prince George Alexander Louis of Cambridge was born in a London hospital. The baby was named for Queen Elizabeth's father and grandfather. The bells of Westminster Abbey chimed for three hours in celebration.

The little prince was immediately the center of media attention. The day after his birth, hundreds of photographers waited outside the hospital to snap the first pictures of the littlest royal.

After George's birth, Catherine took a break from working for nine months. Her first stop after leaving the hospital was Bucklebury to stay with her parents. Here, the duke and duchess were able to relax out of the public eye while getting to know their little boy.

William made changes, too. Two months after George's birth, the duke left the Royal Air Force. He wanted to concentrate on royal duties and charity events with his wife.

Both William and Catherine took a break from work to spend time with baby George.

Family on the Go

As the future king, George will grow up in the public eye. When he was just nine months old, he took his first official tour with his mother and father. The family traveled to New Zealand and Australia, where they stayed for three weeks. During the trip, His Royal Highness visited zoos and had playdates with other babies. When he got tired, his nanny took him home.

Catherine and her family arrive at Wellington, New Zealand.

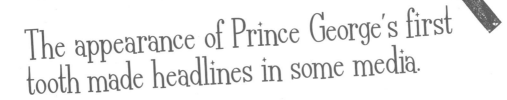

The appearance of Prince George's first tooth made headlines in some media.

Catherine works hard to help her son balance his time in the spotlight with a more private, normal lifestyle. After the Australia trip, people praised the duchess for being a hands-on mother. She carried George everywhere and even played with him on the floor. Many people compare her parenting style with William's mother, Diana.

Catherine talks with children at Harlem's Northside Center for Child Development in New York City.

In 2014, readers of a fashion Web site chose Catherine as Britain's most stylish woman.

In September 2014, William announced that Catherine was pregnant for the second time. The baby, a girl born on May 2, 2015, is fourth in line to the throne.

Even before the baby's birth, the future royal family member was subjected to media attention. Within months of the announcement, reporters were publishing photos of Catherine's growing stomach online and in newspapers.

One day, Catherine will become Queen Catherine, consort of King William V. She has big shoes to fill. The current royal consort, Prince Philip, is patron of hundreds of organizations. Before him, Queen Elizabeth II's mother helped inspire the nation during World War II (1939–1945).

Until then, Catherine continues her work for the queen and for charity. She also does her best to give her family as normal a life as possible, while preparing for the challenges ahead. ★

Catherine and William named their daughter Princess Charlotte Elizabeth Diana.

True Statistics

Catherine's official title: Her Royal Highness Duchess Catherine of Cambridge, Countess of Strathearn, and Lady Carrickfergus

Date Catherine was born: January 9, 1982

Place Catherine was born: Reading, England

Name of Catherine's parents: Michael and Carole Middleton

Name of Catherine's siblings: Philippa (b. 1983); James (b. 1987)

Name of Catherine's husband: William, Duke of Cambridge (b. 1982)

Schools Catherine attended: Marlborough College (1996–2000); University of St. Andrews (2001–2005)

Did you find the truth?

Kate Middleton left university to marry Prince William.

Kate's son George will one day become king of the United Kingdom.

Resources

Books

Bryan, Dale-Marie. *William and Kate*. Mankato, MN: The Child's World, 2013.

Kling, Andrew A. *The British Monarchy*. Detroit: Lucent Books, 2012.

Zeiger, Jennifer. *Queen Elizabeth II*. New York: Children's Press, 2015.

Visit this Scholastic Web site for more information on Kate Middleton:
★ www.factsfornow.scholastic.com
Enter the keywords **Kate Middleton**

Important Words

buyer (BYE-ur) — someone whose job is to select items for clothing and other stores

charity (CHAR-uh-tee) — an organization that raises money to help people in need or some other worthy cause

commoner (KAH-muhn-ur) — a person who is not royalty

consort (KAHN-sort) — a husband or wife of the ruling monarch

media (MEE-dee-uh) — members of a group whose job is to communicate with large numbers of people

monarchy (MAH-nur-kee) — a government in which the head of state is a king or queen

paparazzi (pah-puh-RAHTZ-ee) — photographers who take pictures of famous people for money

patron (PAY-truhn) — a person who gives money to or helps another person or a cause

representative (rep-ri-ZEN-tuh-tiv) — someone who is chosen to speak or act for others

tiara (tee-AHR-uh) — a small jeweled crown worn by women

yacht (YAHT) — a large boat or small ship with sails, used for pleasure or for racing

Index

Page numbers in **bold** indicate illustrations.

About the Author

Robin S. Doak has been writing for children for nearly 25 years. A graduate of the University of Connecticut, Doak loves writing about history makers from the past and the present. She lives in Maine with her family.